Encounter

Linda Dobinson

Copyright © 2015 Linda Dobinson

All rights reserved, including the right to reproduce this book, or portions thereof in any form. No part of this text may be reproduced, transmitted, downloaded, decompiled, reverse engineered, or stored, in any form or introduced into any information storage and retrieval system, in any form or by any means, whether electronic or mechanical without the express written permission of the author.

ISBN: 978-1-326-11617-0

PublishNation, London
www.publishnation.co.uk

Contents

Barbados Nights	1
High Tide	2
Accra Sunset	3
Dawn	4
I need you in my life	5
Holding On	6
Frozen	7
Promises and Rings	8
Love	9
Stain	10
Thorns	11
Leaving	12
Reflections	13
Memories	14
Saturday Night At The Disco	15
Encounter	16
The Girl	17
Journeys On The 7.20	18
Last Summer	20
Pictures	21
Glass	22
Daybreak	23
Sunset	24
The Seasons	25
Spring Villanelle	26
A Spring Day	27
Summer Villanelle	28
Roundabout	29
Autumn Villanelle	30
An Autumn's Day	31
Rain	32
Winter Villanelle	33

Snow	34
Happy	35
Listen to the wind	36
Summer Storm	37
Disco	38
September	39
October	40
November	41
Winter Is Wonderful	42
A Quiet Night	43
Spring sits upon a cloud	44
Here Comes Spring	45
Swifts	46
A Rainy Day In Basingstoke	47
A wisp of wind	48
Rainy Day	49
Mist	50
Winter Days	51
White Winter's Night	52
A Spring Day	53
Spring Snow	54
A Perfect Summer's Day	55
On blue days	57
The Garden	58
Autumn	59
Autumn (2)	60
21 December	61
The Christmas Season	62
Mindscape	63
The Prisoner	68
Alone	69
Time	70
Lost Dreams	71
Stray thoughts	72

Change	73
Tea Break	74
DIY	75
Red Hearts Rule On A Saturday Night	76
Words	77
I want to write	78
Footprints In The Sand	80
Schooldays	81
October Child	82
Girl In The Park	83
Sophie	84
The Path	85
A Walk	86

Barbados Nights

A full moon shines in the starry sky
picking out highlights on the breakers.

Accra's powder sand sifts between my toes,
the surf laps around my ankles.

This is the time you come to me-
when the beach belongs to us alone.

This is the time our laughter rides the wind –
as we dance to the calypso beat.

This is the time *Mount Gay* rum makes us glow -
as the Trade Wind fans the flickering fire.

This is the time we are at one with nature-
roaring to the rhythm of the waves.

This is a time that exists for us alone-
when I call to you and you come to me.

High Tide

Beneath a soft silver moon
the soft silver sand of Accra beach
holds the secrets and footprints
of those whose paths have lead them here.
At high tide the far reaching waves
will wipe away the footprints of the day
but the secrets will always remain.

By the light of the wandering moon
a young woman is humming a love tune
as she walks in the surf. The warm salty air
plays with her long black hair.
As she swings her arm gold bangles jangle
from her fingers sandals dangle.
Fine foamy drops of spray sprinkle
the hem of her flowing white skirt.

By the light of the watchful moon
a young man strums a love tune
on his guitar as he sits in the sand.
He looks up – there she stands.
She blows a kiss as she drops to her knees
with a pout designed to tease.
He replies with a grin that is welcoming.
Enticingly she holds out her hand,
he abandons his guitar – she has her man.
As the waves wash towards the lonely guitar
and they are fanned by the warm salty air
the moonlight simmers in her long blond hair.

Accra Sunset

When the day is ending and the tourists
drift away, I like to sit on the beach
and watch the sun's slow descent.
As the searing heat subsides, sea breeze
cools, fills my nose with briny scent.

In front of me the restless Atlantic,
wave after wave crashing and foaming
on to the beach, then quietly receding -
energy spent.

Today, idly sifting sand between my fingers
feeling the grains as they flow,
I muse over the ocean's permanence
and love's transience.
But the beauty of the scene is powerful,
it fills my mind and soul - I laugh.
Perhaps, instead, I should compare love to the waves -
there will always be another!

One strong wave washes high on to the beach,
I follow it back to the water's edge.
Wet sand squelches between my toes
as I splash in the surf - I'm contented.

The golden sky deepens and darkens,
flickering stars appear
as the sun sinks beneath the sea.
Yes, I like to stroll on the beach
when the day is ending
and the tourists drift away.

Dawn

Dawn's thin light creeps
around the room awakening me.

Taking me away
from my dreams - from you.

All I have left of you
are dreams. Only in dreams

can I touch you, hold you,
walk with you along the shore

of Accra beach. The white sand,
the rolling Atlantic waves -

Accra beach, our beach at midnight
when there was only us,

us and the friendly moon.
I remember the smell of the salty air

mixed with the scent of you.
The scent of you - sweeter than the rose

that climbs beneath my window,
now blushed with dew in the dawn.

I need you in my life

I need you in my life
like a river needs the rain
ever since I met you
the world's made sense again.

You're the one that I turn to
you pick me up when I am down
and when the tears are flowing
you're the smile to my frown.

You're the surf around my feet,
you're the sea spray on my face
and when the sun is setting
you're the star that takes its place.

You're the substance to my shadow,
you're my bright light in the dark
and when the night is ended
in the morning you're my lark.

You're the first word on my lips,
you're the last word on my page
and when the story's over
the memories will not fade.

I need you more than sunshine
more than the birds need the trees
please hold my hand real tight now
let us share our destinies.

Holding On

Love is just a game we like to play
but deep inside we know it doesn't mean much -
you're not my knight in shining armour
and I'm aware I'm not your maiden fair.
But right or wrong we're holding on.

Maybe someday you will leave me,
or it might be me who does the walking out –
who knows, who knows. And if we part
would our time together even matter?
But for now we're holding on.

Then again, you're always there,
I know that I can rely on you.
It may not be a torrid affair
but then again, passion can change like fashion.
So we're holding on to what we got.

Frozen

We stepped out the door into a still night.
The sudden cold froze our laughter - briefly,
only briefly. Then your lips found mine
and the cold was forgotten.
It had been a good night, nothing
out of the ordinary- just a good night.
The Mercury Inn - a favourite pub,
a meeting place. It had been crowded -
as usual, smoky - as usual, from red tipped
cigarettes. We didn't mind the smoke, back then
it was just - atmospheric. You drank your beer,
I drank my *Babycham*. We had a couple of goes
on the pool table. Like I said -
nothing out of the ordinary.
Soon, too soon, it was last orders
and the long walk home.
There was little traffic - once the initial rush was over.
No other walkers - we had the sidewalk to ourselves.
I leaned on you, you hugged me close.
No one read body language back then.
A few crystal stars pricked the black sky,
snowflakes crunched like broken glass.
Broken glass - why do we break what we can see?
That night, I remember, we were happy,
somewhere between 'I do' and divorce.

Promises and Rings

Promises and rings
seem like precious things.
A ring has no beginning
or no end
and a promise should
never be broken.

But promises and ring
may not be precious things.
A promise is a whisper
on the wind
that blows through the hollow
in the ring.

Love

Love is like a beautiful flower
trailing in a garden bower
sweetening the world with its scent.

At first it is like the delicate bud
vulnerable to everything that could
or would destroy its early promise.

Then its petals unfolds one by one
with every day getting strong
until it reaches the peak of perfection.

Yes love is like a beautiful flower
trailing in a garden bower -
it blooms and fades.

Stain

Red rose petals stain
the frosty lawn like lipstick
on your shirt collar.

Thorns

Bouquet of flowers
wrapped in cellophane and bows,
all I feel are thorns.

Leaving

Lying on this bed
these crumpled sheets

beads of sweat glisten
on my forehead.

The unforgiving moon -
torch bright.

Turning my head
from the light

I hear the door click -
you're leaving.

Reflections

The evening sunshine fills the room,
there's no one here but you and I .
A stray sunbeam falls on your face,
you catch it, throw it at me.
Your smile, seared in my memory,
beams out like so many times before
enticing one back from me.
I wish I could ask you to explain
my place in your scheme of things?
But what would be the use? I'd only hear
what I wanted to hear, the deceived
are often party to their own deception.
Enough, enough! I put you back
on the mantel before you fade.

Memories

I thought of you today
like yesterday and the day before.
I imagined your smile
and the sound of your knock on my door.

I remembered the spring
when we met, the world was fresh and new.
Those exciting first days
I only wanted to be with you.

I recalled the summer
when our love and bodies were entwined.
Those long hot lazy days
I had nothing but you on my mind.

Too soon came the autumn
colours changed, leaves began to fall.
I knew you were busy,
I forgave when you forgot to call.

Those cold days of winter
finally I saw they matched your heart.
My eyes had been opened
our love had been your game from the start.

Saturday Night At The Disco

I lose myself in the disco beat.
Smoke curls and drifts out of sight,
The rhythm takes control of my feet,
The strobe lighting glitters bright.

Smoke curls and drifts out of sight.
Your nearness sets my blood on fire,
The strobe lighting glitters bright,
You have awakened my desire.

Your nearness sets my blood on fire
Let us take it to the extreme.
You have awakened my desire
Tomorrow, tonight will be a dream.

Let us take it to the extreme.
The music thunders in my ears.
Tomorrow, tonight will be a dream
Nothing is what it appears.

The music thunders in my ears,
The rhythm takes control of my feet.
Nothing is what it appears.
I lose myself in the disco beat.

Encounter

We stand face to face
eyes saying words
that mouths cannot.
Wanting yet hesitant.
The world stops –
becomes irrelevant.
Desire rips through my heart
splintering into every cell
in my body.
I know nothing about you,
yet I feel I know you –
what you need,
what makes you tick.
Something clicks,
hesitant becomes urgent.
I want what I should not have,
what I will never
be allowed to keep.

The Girl

The river wanders
by in lazy fashion,
tickled by the stones
sleeping on the bed,
without a care

for the passing
of time. Stretched out
on the bank, toes dipping
in the water, she dreams
romantic dreams untroubled,

as yet, by the shadow
of experience. Love
is like a current trend
that lasts no longer
than the first Beaujolais wine.

Journeys On The 7.20

If I were the sun
and you were the moon
I would shine my light
on your sweet face
and you would feel my warmth.

If I were the sun
and you were the moon
no longer would I stand still
your love would make me spin.

If I were the sun
and you were the moon
no rain would ever fall on us
the way it does on little Earth.

If I were the sun
and you were the moon
nothing on Earth could keep us apart,
not even the Earth itself.

If I were the sun
and you were the moon
we could roam the universe
and the un-crossed stars
would light up our path.

If I were the sun and you were the moon.

But I am not the sun
and you are not the moon.
We are just two people

in separate orbits.
Our worlds touch daily but softly,
so softly that you do not feel it.

I am not the sun
and you are not the moon
So I will have to dream
starry dreams of our journey
through the universe
and all the things we would see and feel
if I were the sun
and you were the moon.

Last Summer

Nose pressed to the glass
she stared into the distance - searching.
The light was fading slowly
and as the long shadow
of the mountain grew darker
it was becoming harder to see
the plain country girl
shepherding her flock of goats
back to the pretty, old village.

The door opening made her turn sharply.
Silently he went to the bar.
Taking the offered glass,
she had no shadow of doubt about his decision.
Lightly shaking her blond hair she stared
at her reflection in the mirror -
so unlike that girl who carried his child.
Soon a plane would carry her over,
for the last time, the mountain so sombre.

Pictures

The clock in the hallway chimes,
briefly the pictures on the TV screen
come to life.
The glass and air from the open door
give her solace,
huddled in her chair
staring out into the night.

Through the window of the cosy café
she saw them - a picture of happiness,
perched on the edge of their seats
almost nose to nose.
She watched for as long as she could bear,
then turned to face the moonlight
and the cicada's song.

Glass

The plane's lights wink in the sky.
Below, the cold air pricks her cheeks
as she leans on the wall of the bridge
staring at a photograph
which in the shadowy night
looks more like a negative.
Moonbeams descend to consort
with the river in friendly fashion,
reflecting on its glassy surface.

A clock strikes twelve, immediately
the sky is filled with colour and noise.
The spectacle cheers her
and making a sudden decision
she tosses the picture into the river.
Leaving her lonely mountain
she bends her steps
towards the pretty glass beads
exploding in the sky.

Daybreak

Darkness imperceptibly less,
yet a single song is sung.
Soon the chorus follows on
welcoming a brand new dawn.

Sunset

At the setting of the sun
a lone bird sings evensong.
The distant traffic's roar and hum
becomes his orchestra.
As darkness overtakes the day
the tools of toil are put away.
Families rush to reunite
and share their day's adventures.

The Seasons

What are the seasons
but paintings on Nature's canvas
exhibited by curator Time
in a repeating cycle.

Spring Villanelle

Hurrah, spring is in the air at last,
people can smile instead of frown
now winter's grasp is no longer fast.

After long months of an arctic blast
snowdrops not snowflakes carpet the ground.
Hurrah, spring is in the air at last.

Fleecy lambs gambol on the lush grass,
bright coloured crocuses will soon abound
now winter's grasp is no longer fast.

'Neath the sun dancing shadows are cast
from tiny new leaves the breeze has found.
Hurrah, spring is in the air at last.

Bees on the nectar trail float pass,
happy birds are singing all around
now winter's grasp is no longer fast.

The new spring collection will be vast
so I'm on the bus and heading to town.
Hurrah, spring is in the air at last
now winter's grasp is no longer fast.

A Spring Day

A snowfall of daisies
covers the grassy verges
where magpies, dressed in best bib and tucker,
strut their stuff.

Summer Villanelle

The sun shines bright over Basingstoke town,
Zephyr tickles the leaves on the trees
as the shadows set free dance all around.

Starlings swoop down for the worms to be found,
cats stretch out lazily and scratch their fleas.
The sun shines bright over Basingstoke town.

People drawn from their houses abound,
some tend their gardens to the hum of bees
as the shadows set free dance all around.

Some go to the match at the Camrose ground,
'The Blues' do their best their fans to please.
The sun shines bright over 'Basingstoke Town'.

Children have fun at their local playground
flying on swings or throwing frisbees
as the shadows set free dance all around.

But it is to the pub that I am bound,
a G&T will do nicely for me.
The sun shines bright over Basingstoke town
as the shadows set free dance all around.

Roundabout

The big grassy roundabout
in Basingstoke

with the ring
of evergreen trees

is an oasis
to smoky grey woodpigeons

that never notice when I go by
on the shiny blue bus.

Autumn Villanelle

The temperature plummets like a falling stone
and days are shortened by lengthening night.
How I wish I were in a tropical zone.

The north wind makes a threatening moan
so I draw my coat around me tight.
The temperature plummets like a falling stone.

A mizzling rain soaks me to the bone
and my eyes are dazzled by cars' headlights.
How I wish I were in a tropical zone.

My garden will soon be overblown
by falling leaves that have given up the fight.
The temperature plummets like a falling stone.

Migratory swifts have now all flown
to places where the sun shines bright.
How I wish I were in a tropical zone.

As Christmas approaches and friends abroad phone
summer days are now far out of sight.
The temperature plummets like a falling stone.
How I wish I were in a tropical zone.

An Autumn's Day

Driven by the wind
shapes of grey
sail by like smoke
constantly swirling and transforming.

Fat drops of rain
are hurled to the ground
their wetness explodes
seeping into every pore and crevice.

While leaves of gold and green
are ripped from trees
unable to resist the force,
their naked beauty now exposed.

Rain

Pitter patter pitter patter
rolling down the rooftops.
Pitter patter pitter patter
drumming the double glazing.
Pitter patter pitter patter
pounding the pavement.
Pitter patter pitter patter
disappearing down the drain.

Winter Villanelle

I love to go walking on a winter's night
the sky is full of stars not bats,
when a waxy moon is shining bright.

Nature has dusted the world in white
capturing the prints of prowling cats.
I love to go walking on a winter's night.

The glimpse of an owl in silent flight
keen eyes searching for mice and rats,
when a waxy moon in shining bright.

The orange glow from a streetlight
reflecting on the deserted tarmac.
I love to go walking on a winter's night.

It's fun to have a snowball fight
with a smiling snowman who is round and fat,
when a waxy moon is shining bright.

Looking around the world's alright,
so snug in my boots and my bobble hat
I love to go walking on a winter's night
when a waxy moon is shining bright.

Snow

Fragile

                                              flakes

                fall

                                from

the

                  sky

          and settles
        on the rooftops
like icing on a gingerbread house.

Happy

Happy is spring all green and warm
floating on the air like a bumble bee.
Happy are bees scouring for nectar
to make honey for you and me.
Happy are flowers popping out of the ground
shouting their colours for all to see.
Happy are chicks cosy in the nest
soon they will grow and be flying free.
Happy are the trees no longer bare
they give the birds a sanctuary.
Happy am I now spring is here
opening a new world of possibilities.

Listen to the wind

Listen to the wind
as it tears through trees
and around the houses upsetting wheelie bins.

Feel the wind
as it caresses your face making cheeks red
and re-combs your hair.

Smell the wind
freshly washed by rain.
See the rain through speckled lenses.

Summer Storm

Lighting flashing
thunder crashing
rain lashing
children splashing
in the growing puddles.

Wind whipping
brollys flipping
people slipping
water dripping
off of everything.

Trees swaying
wheels spraying
fences shaking
traffic snaking
through the soggy curtain.

Then flashes start to fade,
black clouds for creamy clouds trade,
fat drops no longer pervade,
golden beams cascade.
The storm is moving on.

Disco

On hot summer nights
see disco lights, feel the beat,
let yourself go - dance.

September

The mid-september day dawns fair
many leaves still cover the trees

as green as when they first unfurled.
But in the air I can feel
that winter waits within the wings.

Summer jeans and summer t-shirt
covered by an autumn jacket,
a pleasant stroll to my bus stop.

I'm off to the bright lights of the shops.
Each new season brings new fashion
which I'll follow with a passion.

October

As I look up to the sky
I see cloud on layered cloud go by
hunted eastward by the wind.

The garden chairs look forlorn
now relieved of the weight they'd bourn –
time that they were put away.

A few late flowers still remain
encouraged by autumn rain –
salvia thinks it is summer still.

But other plants are settling down
as cold now penetrates the ground
and frosts cannot be far away.

I'm looking for that pesky bee
that would not let the flowers be
all summer long – but he's now gone.

November

Yellow geranium leaves
look bright against

the tall green grass
sprinkled with dew drops

that sparkle like diamonds
in the early morning sun.

Winter Is Wonderful

A winter's morn cold and clear
warm breath hangs on the air
for a moment, then disappears.
Jack Frost tickles nose and toes
all trace of slumber quickly goes.
Trees surreal in skeletal beauty
limbs reach out in graceful serenity.

Long delicious exciting nights
a heady mix of dark and street lights.
Darkness hides dirt and imperfections,
pools of light encourage reflections.
Moon and stars come out to greet
the lights of man which can't compete
with their beauty and mystique.

A Quiet Night

A candle wax moon
slips across the night sky.
Stars like scattered diamonds
prick the darkness.
All is quiet.
The day's strong wind
has blown itself away
taking the rain with it.
All that's left are a few puddles
shimmering in the moonlight.

Spring sits upon a cloud

Spring sits upon a cloud
surveying the scene
and biding her time.
I sit on the sofa
surveying the clouds
waiting for spring to descend.

Here Comes Spring

Here come the leaves
one by one
covering the anorexic trees
with their greenness.

Here come the flowers
one by one
filling the fresh spring air
with their exquisite scent.

Here comes the sun
the one and only
no longer keeping its distance.

Swifts

For me summer arrives with the swifts.
With beautiful slim curved wings
they swoop low, soar high, move faster
than any other bird can fly
their distinctive cry
carried on the wind.

Then as suddenly as they came
they are gone moving on
across the sea a long journey
for the new generation.
For me the best of summer
goes with the swifts.

A Rainy Day In Basingstoke

A leaden sky inspires contemplation.
Flowers are sent into a desperate dance
as Boreas roves restlessly without cessation.
I view it all from my window entranced.

Flowers are sent into a desperate dance
to the music of a leafy rustle.
I view it all from my window entranced.
The slanting rain makes people scuttle.

To the music of a leafy rustle
I grab my coat and run out of doors.
The slanting rain makes people scuttle.
Boreas and I need no one more.

I grab my coat and run out of doors,
thunderclouds clap and produce a flash.
Boreas and I need no one more.
I dance in puddles that make a splash.

Thunderclouds clap and produce a flash
as Boreas roves restlessly without cessation.
I dance in puddles that make a splash.
A leaden sky inspires contemplation.

A wisp of wind

A wisp of wind whirls
fallen leaves as summer slips
into memory.

Rainy Day

Blue chinks are glimpsed
then gone
as clouds hurry, scurry,
curl and swirl.

Leaves past their prime
rustle loudly
as they are ruffled roughly
by the wind.

Rain at first a fine mist
suddenly turns
more substantial
pattering and patterning windows.

Soon pools grow
collecting and reflecting
distorted images
through repeating ripples.

Whilst unseen birds
find something to sing about.

Mist

Cold and gloomy dawns the autumn morn
on the air hangs a heavy mist
that touches like a lost love's kiss.

A thin light glimmers from a street lamp
reflecting on the persistent damp.

Shining bright through the hazy vapour
are leaves as yellow as summer sun,
yet, like tears, they will fall one by one.

This moment now frozen in memory
will swiftly pass into history.

Winter Days

       i
Cold air grates the face,
a gloom taps the attention.
Hurried clouds fifty shades of grey.
Dusty memories their shadows cast,
brown dry leaves are blown past.

      ii
The pale blue evening sky
is smudged by small dark grey clouds
as they sail slowly eastwards.

      iii
Another sunless day
not a chink of blue
to alleviate the gloom
that surrounds
like a suit of armour.

      iv
Flurries of snow
have left a thin covering on the road
and given the grass dandruff.
A lone woodpigeon sits on the fence
as a further flurry descends.
Other birds hurry by
dark shapes against the creamy grey sky.

White Winter's Night

It has fallen all day long
the roofs and sky are as one.
The pavements and street sparkle bright
no tyre tracks or footprints mar the white.

Heavy laden plants outside of homes
struggle to support their mushroom domes.
But bare branches now fat with snow
still offer a perch to pigeon, magpie and crow.

Cold nose, cold toes and cold fingers
yet this arctic wonderland makes me linger.
I want to catch a snowflake in the palm of my hand.
I want to build a big fat snowman.
I want to make footprints in the snow.
I want to get on my sledge and go go go.

Then when I am tired and cold to the bone.
I'll gladly go back to my gingerbread home
and snuggle down in my big soft bed
and pull the duvet right over my head
and think about my lonely snowman
and hope tomorrow he won't be gone.

A Spring Day (2)

Winter did its best to make us freeze
and succeeded admirably,
but now the time has come
for cold dull days to be gone.
It is spring – officially. But who would know it?
Snow not spring drifts on March's winds.
Sugar cube roofs and fondant topped cars.
Glace roads and sugar sprinkled grass.
Caster sugar trees and icing sugar plants.
Piped icing fences and vanilla ice cream sky.
All very pretty. I've had enough.
The only white I want to see is March's lamb.
Oh let this be winter's last big roar
so timorous spring can come at last.

Spring Snow

It's snowing, it's snowing
the breeze is blowing
flakes are hurled to the ground.
The birds are hiding
but the trees are siding
with the wind as it whirls all around.

A Perfect Summer's Day

On a perfect summer's day
a blue painted sky
stretches from horizon to horizon.
The warmth of the sun
draws people from their houses,
so many things can now be done.

A day at the seaside, sand and surf.
Laze on the beach and catch a tan,
the gentle plash of waves
will make all stress fade away.

Of course that's not all that might fade away.
The sun can make life fade away
as melanomas grow to take fair skin's place.

A picnic in the country.
Air pollution free smells so sweet.
Happy birds sing and swoop,
food shared with friend tastes so good.

Of course wasps like a picnic too,
if you do not share with them
they might share their anaphylactic sting with you.

Sit in the garden.
Read a book, sip some wine
the flowers are blooming
everything is fine.

Of course the lovely summer breezes
carry pollen which bring sneezes
streaming eyes and the wheezes.

At the end of a perfect summer's day
gentle night wearing a crown of silver stars
settles down to rule.
With pools of moonlight
and benevolent breezes it brings relief.
Windows are left open to let Zephyr in.

Of course that is not all that comes in.
A spider black as night scuttles in
and secretes itself in a dark corner, waiting
to greet you on some other perfect summer's day.

On blue days

On blue days when the sleepy breeze
rocks the red roses scattering scent,
I sit on the weathered timber bench
remembering the blue of your eyes.

The Garden

Shiny sycamore leaves
fan warm air
over the garden,
while dandelions vie
for space once occupied
by deckchairs and sun lotion.

Autumn

Autumn breezes in and Summer is ousted.
She brings with her a new palette of colour,
shades of sienna and gold she unfolds,
but her gold is fools gold, a flash-in-the-pan,
Winter's lackey she sets decay in motion.

Autumn (2)

Another September.
The end of another summer.
Hot days long as dreams
when every dream seemed possible.
Now a sudden cold fills the air
and dreams shrink with the days.

Another October.
The mid-autumn sun shines warm.
Little red berry jewels
accessorize the dull green leaves.
In the air a stillness-
a pause in the transition
from summer to winter.

Another November to remember.
Night grows bolder by the day,
day becomes more changeable.
This morning's grey gave way
briefly to beautiful blue.
Then clouds returned to look down
on an explosion of yellow leaves
that carpet the ground.
Branches now thin and bare
look like spent sparklers
waving in the air.

21 December

A grey day, mild, a gentle breeze.
The hum of the morning traffic
in the distance mixes with the call
of birds flitting from roof top
to roof top, from tree to tree
searching for berries and bread.
The row of spiny limbs that interlock
making a lacy pattern against the sky
is interrupted by a few yellow-brown
leaves that cling on waiting
for one strong puff to blow them off.
The overnight rain is drying
just a few specks dot the windows
and a few small pools are left on the road.

The Christmas Season

As the long winter nights settle on the land
the lights of man shine out
keeping the darkness at bay.
Well wrapped against the cold with out
we search for the warmth within
each other and our selves
at this special time of year.
Up and down the land joyful music blares out
gladdening hearts and loosening tongues
as we cannot help but sing along.
Loved ones across the miles are brought near
by words carried in the sacks of postmen
and down telephone wires.
Young minds are enthralled
as the myth of Santa Claus is handed down
while older ones ponder on deeper meanings.

Mindscape

Echo

The cirrus clouds are edged in gold
by the setting sun.

Through a field a couple are walking,
in the distance their friends are waiting.
A row of oak trees edge the field,
on a branch a lone bird sings.

I pause, and look, but cannot see it.

The midsummer evening is warm
and still. The leaves on the trees hang
like sleeping bats.
Beneath the tree a man is sitting,
obscured by the shadows - he watches.

A distant church bell starts to ring,
the couple stop - they can hear it.

In the distant village is a pub - The Old Bell.
For a hundred years a fire has burned
a welcome in its hearth for all who come.
When it is quiet you can hear the echo
of revellers past.

Softly whistling the man rises
and walks away.

The lone bird pauses his twilight song.

A cat prowls among the grass,
the couple try to coax it to them
but it darts away - afraid of strangers.

It climbs the oak tree,
a dark silhouette against the dusky sky.
It pauses, watches me, I keep walking.

The sound of the bell -
only an echo now.

<u>Falling</u>

Summer faded. Now
its vibrant colours are no more
than a picture in my memory. The world

is grey, the way it looks
when you dream. From my window
I can see the grey. Days

pass. Each new day
a photocopy of the previous,
like stones in a wall.

From my window I see the trees
are still - like time stopped.

Yet high in the sky the birds still soar,
casting pale shadows on the earth
and calling as if to say-
'none of this makes any difference to us'.

From my window I see them soar
and the doors of houses
shut fast.

In the distance a low growl of thunder echoes.
Eventually the rain comes, cold drops
striking the earth before being absorbed.

I cry too. Hot drops
trickling down hotter skin
until they reach the precipice
of my cheeks - then falling.

And still the days are grey,
tears can never wash away the grey
or smooth the jagged edges
that rip and tear.

I look into the future, the present reflects
back at me and I am afraid. Fear
is a lonely emotion.

I remember my school playground.
Under the shadow of tamarind trees,
there was a stone block about ten feet tall
with steps cut into it. The top
was big enough for six children to sit on.

Every morning, before the bell,
we used to play on those steps.
It never entered my head I could fall.

I wonder if it is still there
or if the school has knocked it down,

finally afraid a child might fall.

Another day has spent its time
and now quietly leaves the scene.

Dream

A new day stretches over the horizon
soaking up the darkness like a sponge.

The day is a blank page.
Anything is possible for those
brave enough to make of it what they will.

For me, like many others, each new day
is just another round of coffee and paper clips,
office gossip and rush hour traffic.

Yet we tell ourselves our jobs are important
and our lives full, when we are no more than dots
on the pointillist painting called life.

Yet at night I go home to Russell.
With the spiky red hair, with the green eyes,
with a mouth that is always close to a smile.
Who never takes anything seriously,
who never analyses anything, who makes me laugh.

Last night I had a dream.

I dreamed I was in a deserted
car park surrounded by a wire fence.
I was standing to one side,

with the fence close behind me.

The concrete floor was white
instead of the usual dull grey. It was daytime,
the bright sunlight highlighted
the white.

I didn't know why I was there,
or how I got there.

Suddenly, on the opposite side,
a large Doberman appeared.
It started running towards me.
I was terrified, I could not move.

When it reached me it put its mouth
around my hands, I could feel its teeth on my skin.
It didn't bite, but I knew I dare not move.

The 'beep beep beep' of the alarm
interrupted the silence.
Cat gazed at me sleepily
as I reached out and turned it off.

The Prisoner

A prisoner stands by a window,
the world outside is all aglow.
Lights beam forth full and bright,
heralding the coming of the night.
Another day has come and gone,
another day of seeing no one.
Creatures are coming out to play
now they can have it all their own way.
The moon slips gently into sight
bathing the world with its soft light.
The prisoner stands and watches it all
locked inside her own four walls.
Why she's there no one knows
but every day her discontent grows.

Alone

I stand alone.
The room is dark.
My slightly opened window
lets in the sound of the traffic
from the distant motorway,
and the breeze which flutters
the rose-patterned curtain.
Lights shine out
from behind windows and doors,
the bright street lights
shine out even more
casting a floral shadow
on the wall behind me.
Downstairs the sound of the TV
filters up, and the sound
of someone washing up.
Surrounded as I am by light and noise
I stand alone. Lonely. In the dark.

Time

Time is an elusive thing
that no one can hold on to.
It marches on its own sweet way
people drowning in its wake.

Why do we deceive ourselves
that we have so much of it?
Putting off from day to day
all the things we mean to do
from a mixture of laziness and fear.

'Seize the moment' someone said or I read.
'Yeah yeah, tomorrow' I said.
Too many tomorrows became
too many yesterdays I did not seize,
now all that's left are empty memories.

Lost Dreams

Dots of colour
dispersed pointillism
drifting on a sea of memory.
Memory that can scarce remember
how to put them back together again.

Stray thoughts

Stray thoughts like weeds pop
up in my mind destroying
cells of sanity.

Change

I wrote a poem today,
I set it back in time
to the days of my youth
when words did not rhyme.

I dusted off my memories,
the images still had their shine
just as bright as yesterday
when colours did not rhyme.

I summons up the faces
the mists of time enshrined
and all the things we did
when days did not rhyme.

I heard the echo of laughter
like the sound of a clock in chime.
We thought we'd laugh forever
when time did not rhyme.

But nothing lasts forever,
everything passes its prime.
Then one day you will find
everything starts to rhyme.

Tea Break

The house is so quiet.
So quiet that I can hear the wind
howling as it ruffles the trees
which, like upside down besoms,
appear to sweep the sky.
This is my quiet time
when I can enjoy a cup of tea
and a choccy digestive
and not think of all the things
I have to do. But this oasis
of calm passes soon.
I must get back to the real world.

DIY

Slipping sliding dripping gliding-
my paint roller over the wall.

Upwards downwards upwards downwards
new colour overtakes the old.

Of colours to choose so many hues
you can paint yourself a rainbow.

Upwards downwards upwards downwards
I'm getting into the rhythm.

One wall done another begun
the smell of fumes my nose consumes

spotty from spray don't step in the tray.
Upwards downwards upwards downwards.

Red Hearts Rule On A Saturday Night

Red Hearts rule on a Saturday night,
there's plenty food and flagons of ale.
Everyone's happy in the Starlight.

The drummer drums with all his might,
the singer's soft voice tells a tale.
Red Hearts rule on a Saturday night.

Fans join in when the time is right,
up to the rafters their voices sail.
Everyone's happy in the Starlight.

All the girls are looking for a knight,
in killer heels and painted nails.
Red Hearts rule on a Saturday night.

The boys all look for Miss Tonight -
they'll have some tales their friends to regale.
Everyone's happy in the Starlight.

Come along you don't need an invite,
all are welcome at the wassail.
Red Hearts rule on a Saturday night.
Everyone's happy in the Starlight.

Words

Words running through my mind
like a happy band of children
playing hide and seek.
'Catch me if you can'
they seem to shout.
Then all at once
they come tumbling out
on to the page
all of a jumble won't behave.
They have to be coaxed
into rhythm and rhyme.

I want to write

I want to write.
To impress on the page
The thoughts and feelings that rush
Through my mind, up and down my spine.
But on a day like this
When the sky is blue
And through my window
The sun pours in, I yearn to go out.
But not to run through the grass
Or watch the bees harass
The flowers dancing in the breeze
Or admire the swaying trees
Or see anything with a poet's eye
Or feel anything with a poet's soul.
No I feel the pull of the shops.
I want to enter through wide open doors
Into wide open stores
And indulge my passion
For following the latest trend in fashion.
Let me meander to an island in the river
An oasis of calm where I can browse at leisure.
With a little bit of faith
I will find some killer heels.
If I can borrow some money from Aldo
A new handbag will be an easy deal.
Don't you just love to accessorize?
Next, I will follow the gap
And make a French connection
With my friend Morgan who's a pilot
Then we can have a mango
Before the monsoon sets in.
Summers are so hot with Ann.

It's top to shop in a warehouse
To be dazzled by colour and style
To try on designer goodies
And feel like a celeb for a while.
OK, so I am a little kookai!

Footprints In The Sand

Back in the swinging sixties
when I was in my six-to-teens
holes in the ozone
were things unknown
so with bucket and spade
I busily made
castles on Brandon's beach.
As the water there
is calm and clear
with my rubber ring
I splashed in
while the sun beat down
turning me brown
and I laughed and I ran
making footprints in the sand.

Schooldays

'Schooldays are the best days of your life'
my parents said to me
as I dragged on my uniform
and trudged to St. 'Fred's.
The uniform was green and white
the teachers shite
(well maybe not all)
and I hated netball
and going for as run
in the scorching Bajan sun
wasn't much fun.
But now with hindsight
I see my folks were right.
I remember my sunny classroom
with its well-trod wooden floor
and the ringing of the bell
which had us scampering to the door.
I remember my graffitied desk
and my polished chair,
I remember the prefects yelling
'no running on the stairs'.
I remember my old classmates
(well most of them at least)
and sitting under the star apple tree
sharing our lunchtime feast.
I loved that green and white uniform
which showed that I belonged,
I remember my happy schooldays
those innocent times long gone.

October Child

Icy winds stir red and gold leaves
making them flicker like fire.
Between the leaves, spots of smoke-grey sky
are seen by Smartie-brown eyes.
Captivated by the moving colours
a young girl enjoys the solitude.
Her brown hair, cobweb fine,
is being un-plaited by the wind.
Her scarlet coat, bright as the leaves,
is buttoned up fast to keep out the cold.

A red leaf spirals down, her eyes follow it.
Bending to pick it up, she sees a squirrel
scampering along a branch a few yards away.
She freezes. Watching intently as it hops
from branch to branch, she reaches out
with mental fingers to touch its soft grey fur.
It pauses briefly, nose pointing into the air,
then hurries away.

Pocketing the leaf, she presses her small hand
against the trunk of a tree and skips around it,
the rough uneven bark tickling her soft skin.
Small boot-clad feet scatter the dried leaves
that swoosh and crackle with every jump.
Stopping, she raises her eyes again
to the towering trees. Something
cold touches the back of the leg. She turns,
and laughs. Scooping a small brown tabby
into her arms she murmurs - 'OK Tiggy, I'm coming'.

Girl In The Park

It's not the eyes that first you notice
though they are like pools of liquid chocolate
made from the finest cocoa beans.
Nor is it the silky hair that flows
so carelessly around her shoulders.
No, it is her pretty mouth which twitches
with a mischievous smile that first you notice.
The smile that suggests she is happy
but it could be born of memory
and not of anticipation. I wonder.
Her clothes which fit so well
are they designer or supermarket finest?
I don't believe she cares about such things.
She chooses to sit among the flowers
that have popped up on this fine spring day
and not by the river that flows near by –
that would be my choice.
The quiet river that eases along its path,
shadows of leaves swimming
like little fish on its shiny surface.
No, for her it is the unpicked flowers
and the timid birds, and the companionship
of her devoted dog.

Sophie

Sophie sleeps upon the fence.
Small but perfectly formed,
golden fur shining in the sun,
she's more beautiful than any daffodil.
A loner by nature, nature's child.
Behind those gleaming green eyes
is a wisdom far greater than mine.

The Path

Blue sky on an autumn's evening,
sunshine streaming between the houses
lightening up the yellowing leaves
of trees that line the winding path.
The path well-trod by feet well shod
and by soft small silent cat paws.
The path where dog walkers sometimes rush
and wriggly worms can get crushed
under the wheels of bicycles.
The path where schoolchildren chatter
and babies' pram wheels loudly clatter
over the rough uneven surface.
The path used by lingerers
happily dreaming their dreams
and by the hurried constructing thoughts.
The path where autumn leaves will fall
and winter snow will settle.
The path which the spring rain will wash
and the summer sun will dry.
The path for all seasons
used by all for different reasons.

A Walk

A gloomy sky obscures the sun,
shadows are hiding away can't play.
The north wind gives an icy hug,
how I miss my Caribbean days.

The rows of solemn silent trees
like spiny fans against the sky,
not like the flame coloured flamboyant trees
that long ago I once played by.

Barbados was my island home
fourteen years of sea and sun,
tamarinds, drive-in's, panama hats.
warm starry nights made for fun.

Frosty leaves crunch underfoot,
the only sound my ear can hear
as I wend my way along this lonely path,
even the birds have disappeared.

I reach the playground - it's deserted.
The kids have stayed at home,
they have other things to do
on a day like this than roam.

The swing gives a little squeak
as I rock to and fro.
I think of him with whom I swung
not all that long ago.

I married him - I don't know why,
though they do say love is blind.

I should have chose another
when the chance to choose was mine.

Places, faces from the past
I've had enough of memory lane.
Time to leave this lonely place
and head back home again.